TELL YOUR STORY BEFORE THEY DO

TELL YOUR STORY BEFORE THEY DO

*A Guide to Winning the Battle
of You Versus You*

NATE HOWARD

Movement BE Publishing

Tell Your Story Before They Do: A Guide to Winning the Battle of You Versus You

Published by Movement BE Publishing

Copyright © 2021 by Nate Howard

All rights reserved.

Movement BE Publishing
1919 Grand Ave. 2N San Diego, CA 92109
E-mail: nate@movementbe.org

Limit of Liability/Disclaimer of Warranty:

Publishing and editorial team:
Author Bridge Media, www.AuthorBridgeMedia.com
Project Manager and Editorial Director: Helen Chang
Publishing Manager: Laurie Aranda

Library of Congress Control Number:

ISBN: 978-1-7368020-2-1 – softcover
978-1-7368020-3-8 – ebook

Ordering Information:

Quantity sales. Special discounts are available on quantity purchases by corporations, associations, and others. For details, contact the publisher at the address above.

Printed in the United States of America

DEDICATION

I want to dedicate this book to my parents, Harold and Bernice Howard. Thank you for bringing me into this world and being such great supporters in my life. You told me I could do anything—and I believed you.

I also want to dedicate this book to Peggy Crabtree. May your soul RIP. More than being the school's greatest librarian, you were a true champion for us all. I am forever thankful.

CONTENTS

Acknowledgment 9

Introduction 11

Chapter 1   Who Told You? 17

Chapter 2   Identity 29

Chapter 3   Purpose 37

Chapter 4   Intuition 47

Chapter 5   Vision 57

Chapter 6   Resilience 63

Chapter 7   Digital Innovation 73

Chapter 8   Leadership 81

Chapter 9   Sustainability 89

Chapter 10 Wisdom 97

Chapter 11 Closing 105

About the Author 109

ACKNOWLEDGMENT

This book wouldn't be possible without my Movement BE family. I want to send a huge shout-out to all the people who have helped me on this journey. Thank you all for being my biggest supporters from day one. To all the people who have supported but may no longer be with us on this journey—thank you for teaching me the needed lessons for this book.

To all our partners who have helped grow Movement BE from Helix High to San Diego Unified School District and the San Diego County of Education, thank you for believing in us to set a model that we can scale nationwide. Your commitment has created the curriculum that coincides with this book.

And last but not least—a big thank you to Helen Chang, whom I worked collaboratively with during the writing process of this book. Helen, your commitment to helping me tell my story so that I could help others tell theirs is truly remarkable. Thank you so much!

INTRODUCTION

Whose Story Are You Telling?

For so long, people have been trying to tell your story. They've put you in a box. Made you feel less than, and challenged you to live life their way. But you always knew that something felt wrong, that the story they were trying to tell for you was never really yours.

You're tired of being depressed, feeling low about yourself, and having no motivation at all. You're tired of listening to everybody else about what's good for your life. You're tired of feeling stressed out every day, doing school assignments or work that doesn't fulfill you. You want to take control.

You're tired of comparing yourself to others, wanting to be lighter skinned, needing more followers, needing to be appreciated by strangers. You're tired of giving your story away. You're sick and tired of being sick and tired, stressing about your career, the obligations of your family, and how you'll financially provide for yourself for your future.

You're ready to find the courage to accept yourself for who you are, despite what others may think of you, and despite what you sometimes think of yourself. Sometimes it's hard to see your story in who you plan to be, but you've decided to destroy the negative stereotypes that you've reinforced.

You've decided to fight the battle of you versus you and find your true story.

Make It Yours

With the help of this book, you're going to tell a new story—the story that has always been yours, that you've been afraid to write. You'll turn your depression into joy, your pain into purpose, and your stress into productivity, realizing that your story continues the more you write it.

I'm challenging you to enjoy the journey, to embrace your failures, and to understand that being imperfect is just a part of life. You'll have the confidence to determine your own life and the clarity to make decisions that are best for you. As you evolve and grow into the person you were called to be, you'll listen within and realize that you've always had the answer to your story.

Because it's *your* story.

We'll talk about how to forgive yourself for past mistakes, focus on the present moment, and allow yourself to be human. You'll be reminded that it will take hard work, but when you love what you do, you trust the process. You'll realize that your purpose is just your passion connected to your service, connected to the world.

You'll see that in this technological world, we look for value and appreciation in others instead of within ourselves. The goal is to have balance. To understand our connection to social media as a tool to influence, while not being consumed by the need to constantly judge ourselves and compare ourselves to others.

Through the stories on these pages, you'll gain wisdom and understanding about your spiritual essence, realizing that everything comes from within, and that what you shape on the inside reflects what you see on the outside. This full validation of your story will bring you the greatest sense of joy and celebration over your life because you'll have conquered the you-versus-you battle.

This victory will become your greatest joy and your greatest strength. You'll see that adversity is inevitable, and that's okay, because you have the courage to be yourself in a world that doesn't want you to be who you really are. As the attacks continue to come, you'll rejoice over each battle that you win.

It's a Story I Know—Because It Was Mine

My story is no different than yours. I struggled trying to find who I really was. I was living and growing, trying to find my place in the world, trying to find my purpose. Like you, I got tired and frustrated with everybody else trying to tell my story. They wanted to define who I was supposed to be.

Sometimes, circumstances in your life challenge you to make tough decisions. I had to ask myself, *Will I continue living the story that people were writing for me, or will I have the strength and courage to go on my own way?* I made the decision to write my own story, and I never looked back.

Through my passion for poetry and writing, I became the namer of my own story. I founded an organization, Movement BE, to connect with students and help them tell their stories before others do it for them. When I found that this brought me my greatest joy, I stopped subscribing to the story that others were writing for me.

When I really knuckled down and decided to determine my own life, I was surprised to realize that I would be just as happy if millions of people listened to my story or if I were the only one. Because I knew that regardless of what anybody else might say about me, if I were happy with the person within, I would be living the best story ever written.

You want to live your true story? Then come on this journey with me. Let yourself feel the call to trust your intuition, listen to your inner voice, and be more aware of what you're truly called to be.

In each chapter, I'll reveal the themes I learned in my own story that can guide you as you realize them in your own. Read each chapter, one after the other, and take your time as you connect these words to what you're feeling at the moment. This book is meant to be a reminder to reclaim the pen and become the author of your story.

Be Yourself

You truly get what you think about most, so hold this book as the key to the treasure that is your personal story. Are you thinking about your enemy? The one who's trying to write your story? Or are you thinking about yourself, the protagonist, the greatest character ever created? The leader, the hero, the fearless individual whose story will change so many lives?

You are powerful beyond measure. The more you remember this, the more you celebrate this life as a blessing, the more courage you'll have to win the battle within and tell your story. Motivation is a daily reminder, constantly encouraging you to tell your story before *they* do.

But the question always is, Who is *they*?

You'll realize that *they* in the above question is just the you within that has been held back by social injustice, the insecurities of your individuality, or anything else that limits you. You acknowledge this revelation, you accept it, and you tell the story to overcome it. That's where you learn to just *be*.

Thank you for believing in you and picking up this book. Our journey starts now as you begin to write chapter one of your story.

Chapter 1

Who Told You?

The Story of You

From the day you're born, people try to tell your story. Society tells you that you have to be one way. People in your family tell you that you have to be another. You find yourself living a story that you never wrote, one that doesn't speak to the core of who you really are. You find yourself trying to remove parts of your story—or rewrite it altogether.

It doesn't have to be this way.

In searching for your story, you might be tempted to look on the outside, expecting people, places, and things to fulfill the chapters of your book. But everything you discover in your story actually comes from within. The battle for your story is one of you versus you.

The purpose of this book is to remind you that you have the power, and always will, to be the author of your own story. The challenge is for you to realize the power to just be. To *be* means that everything you want . . . you already have.

Through the writing of our stories, we find ourselves as individuals. We find our voices. And when we find our voices, we find our freedom. Taking the time to write our stories, we discover the power to slow down, to share our experiences. When we use the same voices that our oppressors try to silence, our writing becomes the voice of the unacknowledged world. The stories they try to remove from our history uplift and empower us.

Write Your Story from Within

We're often taught in school how to write an argumentative essay, or thesis, or another form of formal writing. But how often are we taught how to write our own personal stories?

Having the courage to write who we are will let us liberate not only ourselves but also countless others. In a world where everyone is trying to tell our stories for us, telling it ourselves is a revolutionary act.

Sometimes our stories have misspellings or bad syntax and grammar. That's okay. Our stories are rough drafts, and we're so hard on ourselves because we think they are final.

But they are not final. That's why this book is challenging you to not let the story die within you. If you can just realize the superpowers that you actually have!

Growing up, I learned that my story was already written for me: go to school, get accepted to a good college, graduate, find a partner, get married, buy a house, and have kids—the American dream. But I was a young Black man growing up in the inner city. I had to write my story within the American dream—not asking for a piece of the pie but taking what was mine.

And that hasn't always been easy. When is it ever?

The Day That Defined Me

In May of 2013, seventy-nine Los Angeles Police Department officers in riot gear showed up at my house.

It was the last day of classes for my last semester at the University of Southern California. I lived in a university neighborhood, and there were two parties on my street that night: one at my house and one right across the street. My party happened to be mostly African American students and students of color. The house across the street had mainly white partygoers.

Parties of one to two hundred people weren't unusual for our college-town neighborhood. We had registered the party with the school; we'd even hired security to keep everyone safe. At around one-thirty in the morning, both parties were in full swing. There had been live music earlier in the night, and now over two hundred college students were at each house, dancing and celebrating the end of the semester.

I was in the backyard at my house, on the DJ stage, speaking to the students, when one of my friends came and tapped me on the shoulder.

"The police are here," he said.

This was pretty normal at USC. Because we were just off campus, it was the LAPD who responded to calls, not campus security. They would tell us to turn the music down, and we would oblige. So I jogged around to the front of the house to meet them.

"Hey, Officers," I said to the three cops standing out front. "I'm Nate Howard, the host of this party."

One of them said, "Hey, we've been getting some noise complaints that your party is too loud."

"Sorry about that! I'll let the DJ know so that we can turn it down."

They nodded, I smiled, and that seemed to be the end of it. We turned the music down, and the party kept going.

About half an hour later, I was up in the DJ booth, taking a turn at the mic, when a different friend tapped me on the shoulder. "Cops again," he said.

I sighed, but I knew the drill. It was 2:00 a.m., probably time to wind the party down anyway. They were just here to shut it down.

I hurried around the side of the house and saw that three cops had already come through the side gate. I wasn't worried. Why would I be? But when none smiled back, I asked, "Hey, what's going on? Is there a need for you to come into our backyard?"

Suddenly, I was thrown against the wall. As my friends clustered around, shocked and confused, handcuffs were slammed around my wrists. It felt like the handcuffs were squeezing my soul, reminding me of my inferiority.

Lights glaring in my eyes blinded me, but I sensed people moving everywhere. I quickly realized those three cops weren't the only ones present. Police in SWAT gear, flashlights and weapons in hand, were raiding the house. Students everywhere were screaming, running. And there was nothing I could do.

The cops shoved me into the back of the police car. Immediately, the noise from outside stopped. I twisted around, my hands pinned behind my back, and stared out the back window.

I remember asking one officer to loosen my handcuffs. He wouldn't budge. Here I was, in the back of this police car, wondering if this was a story that I had to accept—a tired, old story that racially profiled me as a criminal. I tried to fight back with my words, to tell the police that I wasn't a criminal, that I wasn't the stereotype so often identified with young Black men. But I might as well have been speaking to the empty sky.

I sat in the dark of that caged back seat, unable to see or hear what was happening outside. Hour after hour passed. I started speaking my stories and reciting my poetry. I told my stories of oppression, my poetry of injustice. In those moments, I became the master of my story. The hero of my journey.

The officers in the car listened in silence. They didn't say a word.

While I told my stories, the world outside had turned to chaos.

I learned later that the other students were screamed at, pushed, handcuffed by officers. My fellow students were thrown against police cars, knocked to the ground. Some people were hit with batons, bats, and boots. Chaos and confusion escalated into fear and violence. Meanwhile, the party across the street continued.

My White neighbors told TV reporters later that the police had gone to their house and urged them to "stay inside" and "stay safe" while the officers dealt with an "issue" across the street. Our White neighbors were not told to turn down their music or break up their party. None of their White guests were handcuffed.

It was 7:30 a.m. by the time the police car I sat in started to move. I had sat in handcuffs for *five hours*.

The police drove down the block. I thought they were taking me to the police station, but instead, they stopped a block away, parking behind another police car. A third officer came from the other car, walked over to the car I was in, opened the door, and got in my face. He interrogated me about the party, asking about the noise, and told me I was lying about turning the music down. He told me I would receive a citation.

Suddenly, the cuffs were off my wrists, and I was out of the car. I stood there in the morning air, stunned, as they got into two cars and drove away. I walked down that empty street, feeling like a survivor the day after the apocalypse. The sun was rising, and the quiet business of the morning was slowly beginning. At my house, beer cups and other trash littered the backyard.

When I found out from friends that the other house had been left alone, I knew immediately that our house had been targeted for racial profiling. I may have been a USC college graduate, just like my White neighbors, but my degree wasn't visible over the color of my skin.

I opened my door that morning to a reporter who had heard about the altercation and wanted to know more. As our friends posted videos and photos online, I decided to call a protest. By late morning, more and more news stations arrived at my house wanting to interview me, but I told them to meet us at the protest grounds—in front of Tommy the Trojan, a famous school-pride statue at USC.

Most of the students from my party came to protest with me, and we were joined by other students who wanted to support our call for action. At the height of the protest, three hundred students gathered to show their support. I spoke about being a resident of South Los Angeles and the disconnect of having USC as a prestigious university in its backyard. I felt like a visitor on my own campus. That day,

I spoke out about how I felt students of color were treated unfairly. My message became loud and clear.

We organized a town hall that brought together LAPD, students, school administrators, and the community. Seven hundred students arrived to voice our frustrations. A Black officer was the key spokesperson for the panel, and he asked everyone in the room if they thought this was an issue of racial profiling. A sea of seven hundred hands raised high into the air. It was empowering, and it felt like change couldn't help but happen.

The *Los Angeles Times* picked up the story, and I wound up on the front page of countless other newspapers across the nation: a young African American man who protested racial profiling at his university. At first, I was thrilled that my voice was being broadcasted across the country. But soon, I saw that it wasn't the solution to my problem. The media would tell my story, but they wouldn't be able to sustain it. It was part of the news cycle for the week, and then they were on to the next thing. If I wanted to speak up against how I was treated, I would have to keep the story going myself.

To do that, I had to see myself as I truly was, instead of trying to rewrite the story that was written of me. I decided to look at society as a blank canvas. To let go of who they were trying to make me, and just be. I had to learn self-love. I had to win the true battle.

This is what I know: there's no better thing than to sit with yourself and conquer the you-versus-you battle.

People will try to tell us who we are, but we already know. Yes, I'm a young Black man, but what does that mean? Do I create that identity, or do I let someone else create that judgment? Being arrested that night at USC, I felt the struggle of always having to respond to life as a young Black man. Though proud of my culture and the ancestors who fought for me, I will not be limited by society's expectations of me.

I challenge you to do the same.

Despite whatever stereotypes society has placed on you, whether that be race, religion, age, or socioeconomic background, wherever you come from, your story is validated by you. There's no need to force your story. Let it come naturally, and enjoy the journey of life.

You don't have to give your story away to anybody, whether for acceptance or anything else. Through your writing, you can become the namer of your story, truly identifying who you want to be and not allowing others to write the story for you.

A Writing Guide

When things happen unexpectedly, and you're thrown out of your comfort zone, you have only two options: continue to claim the identity that has been a burden to you, or, in the space of uncertainty, write a new story that's connected to your true essence.

This book is a guide to writing that story. It's a rough draft for you to follow on the road to authenticity. You start by examining your identity, learning how to break down the barriers that society has placed on you, using this understanding to become yourself. Then you have to find your purpose. What is the narrative of your story? When your soul ignites, fired up by an unwavering purpose, that's when you know you've found your passion. Once you've found your story and that purpose, trust it. Connect to your intuition, and just be.

Once you start on your way, the way will continue to appear to you, a vision for the future. That's how you begin to tell your story. The struggles will become harder, and the pain may be overbearing. It's through your resilience that you can turn any negative situation into something positive.

That type of critical thinking makes you extremely innovative, turning your pain into your purpose or mission. You'll use your creativity to continue to tell your story through a variety of digital mediums all over the world, inspiring others to tell their stories as well. That's how you're able to be your story.

Great leaders not only tell their own stories, they also create other leaders, inspiring these new leaders to tell their stories as well. That ripple effect is what builds and mobilizes a movement. From there, the essence of the story must be sustained. So we'll talk about financial resources and how to support your vision moving forward.

In the end, in writing our stories, we'll realize we become our greatest teachers. True wisdom is understanding that storytelling has been, and always will be, the essence of how we live our lives. Stories connect us, whether we're swapping tales around the campfire or listening to Grandfather in his rocking chair, telling the stories of his youth.

What story will you pass down? Will you tell it before others try to?

Tell your story before they do. Our lives are filled with magic, and abundance, and prosperity. Often we don't realize we have the choice to tell the stories that we want to tell. Guilt, and peer pressure from others around us, can make us live a miserable and tragic story.

I could have decided to live a story of pain, constantly reacting to those I knew around me. Instead, I took back my identity. I wrote my power.

Now it's your turn.

Chapter 2

Identity

"When you change the way you look at things, the things you look at change."—Wayne Dyer

Who Are You?

Most people don't know their identities.

We're labeled from birth, conditioned into a category that makes it easy for others to identify us. Often we reinforce whatever that label is, whether it's truly us or not.

When we look at racism and stereotypes, we see that much of it comes from the conditioning of identities told to us by other people. That can come from the media, or it can be passed down through generations. It can be a matter of cultural pride. And it can be positive or negative.

For example, take my own identity. The first thing people see about me is the complexion of my skin. They see a Black man. And that identity of Blackness often comes with stereotypes, often comes with assumptions, often comes with a history that was told to me, not one that I discovered myself.

I have pride in my race. Black is what I was raised to be. What I was taught about my Blackness and about where I came from has made me into the person I am today. But at the same time, it's so often used against me. I become limited to an identity that puts me in a collective. And I feel huge pressure if I step out of that box. Either I'm too Black, or not Black enough.

The problem with this identity is that I have something deeper I'm trying to identify with, beyond my outer appearance, on a spiritual level. But for that type of identity, I can't bubble in a mark on a census test. That type of identity can't be represented in data that goes out across the nation or the world to identify the statistics of the certain group I'm supposed to be represented by.

When I was the first person to create a program to help youth identify their stories, I realized that identity is fluid, ever-changing, and evolving. The more you learn about who you really are, then the more you understand that all your experiences up to date have shaped your identity, have given you the power to see who you're truly becoming.

When I'm stereotyped in a specific way, I don't act angry. Instead, I take the time to evaluate and ask myself why it is upsetting me. I know that it's a battle within myself. So often, when others identify and label us in ways that we don't like, we react out of frustration and anger, as if they are the authors of our story. But they only have the power that we give them.

When I battle someone else about my identity, I'm voluntarily giving them my story. I'm asking them to edit and revise it to their liking. Too often, we put the pen in their hands.

It's time to take back our identities.

Ask yourself, *Who do I want to be? How do I want to be defined?* You have to tell your story before they do, and in order to win the battle of you versus you, you have to understand who you are. That means having a clear picture of your own identity, so you can begin to believe in the greatest version of that identity.

We can break identity down into three parts: perception, self-image, and awareness.

Owning Your Perception

The battle with identity is really about perception. The truth is, how we look at others is how we look at ourselves.

We need the courage to see the good in people, to see their best qualities, as we see the best qualities and the goodness within ourselves. We are all struggling with who we are and how we fit into the world. The goal isn't to change who we are to please or fit in with others, but simply to shift our perceptions.

If we all did that, we would all realize we want the same things: love, peace, family, and happiness. All the things that elevate us to our highest selves. The more we practice seeing the world in this way, the more we practice seeing this within ourselves. We can begin to shift and change our identities. And when we do, we shift and change the world at the same time.

Owning Your Self-Image

Malcolm X said, "Who told you to hate your skin? Who told you to hate your hair? Who told you to hate your body in the way you look?"

Your self-image is based on how you identify yourself. It's beyond just your physical appearance. So often, we look at self-image as the complexion of someone's skin, or the way they dress, or their material possessions. The truth is that when you have an understanding of what your self-image is on the inside, everything will match on the outside.

So often, people look to the media or society or other places in the world to find their images, but it's hard to sustain an image that's not truly yours. Eventually, who you're portraying yourself to be will become exhausting, and the mask will fall off.

That's why in Movement BE, we challenge you to just be. Everything becomes natural; everything is authentic. There doesn't need to be a memorized script because it's your story. When you have the courage to be yourself and love your own self-image, you inspire so many other people to do the same.

Awareness Leads to Ownership

We live in our minds most of the day, so we should make them kind places to live. We should be aware of the things that make us feel good, that make us feel like the greatest version of ourselves.

The whole idea of "this is too good to be true," or "I don't deserve this," or "the world is against me" has been conditioned into us from an early age. These programmed phrases kidnap our happiness and take away our joy. We make the negative our default, and then have to force ourselves to get out of that default before we can even try to get to something positive.

Awareness is realizing that that joy, that happiness, could be your default. In practice, it means being aware that we don't have to wait for anything on the outside to make us happy. We can decide right now, with awareness, to go to a positive place.

When I see police brutality in the news and the media, I'm not oblivious to what's happening. I very much know the pain and the struggle that is happening in the world, specifically for young men who look like me, a Black American. But when I wake up in the morning, I also know that it's beautiful outside, that the birds are chirping, that nature is working in great ways. I can begin to be aware of life as I would like to see it because I believe we have to model the world we want to see.

It's about acknowledging our pain and healing through it, but also having the courage to triumph and show the world the stories of what we want to see.

Breaking the Cycle

Identity is all about psychology, but I want to be clear that this doesn't discount real physical dangers. Chokeholds exist; police brutality exists. I've experienced it personally. But I had to realize that I must live the story I want in order to be.

That doesn't mean I'm oblivious or not acknowledging that this is happening. It means that to get beyond race, beyond ideas of discrimination, we have to chart a new story. In that new story, we have to make sure we are inclusive and representative of all, and that the demands for peace are there.

There's a difference between focusing all of my energy on the pain of a life not being here versus having the understanding to mourn, to heal, to write out the pain, and to write that feeling. We need to have the courage and awareness to turn our attention to the lives that are still here, including our own. In that joy, let's work to amplify these other stories so they don't become a hashtag.

Embrace Happiness

So much of my identity as a young man was tied to being this young Black activist. When anything happened that went against the identity of being a young Black man, I didn't know what to do. I felt like I had to be angry to fit that character and identity.

In all truth, if I weren't trying to live this character I thought people saw me as, I could have seen so much sooner what I really wanted, which was joy.

Maybe identity is finding what makes us the happiest. What is our foolish joy and peace? Then, it's about allowing our identity to form a shape around our joy, our love. So often, we think the characters we are living bring us joy. In reality, it's the ego making us temporarily experience joy, temporarily feel pride in who we think we are.

But with ego, we need to be constantly validated. We need to have our accomplishments recognized. And that cycle continues, and we have to keep finding other things to be validated or appreciated for. That gets exhausting.

Instead, our goal should be to find our inner peace, to find our joy. In that infinite space and within those infinite possibilities, we can see that identity can't be any type of label other than to just be.

Chapter 3

Purpose

"When you want something, all the universe conspires in helping you to achieve it." – Paulo Coelho

Poetry with a Purpose

I haven't always known my purpose. In 2013, I was working at my old high school as an academic coach when I decided to create a Be the Voice Poetry Club. On the first day, we had about ten students sign up. They enjoyed poetry and wanted to express themselves creatively.

I thought it was just poetry club. Instead, it became something more than that.

Two weeks later, forty students came to the Be the Voice Poetry Club. We didn't have enough chairs for them all. Nobody told these students they had to stay after school. They came because they were finally seeing a chance to use their voices. Not all of these students were poets, but they were all looking for a safe space to express themselves, to share the stories they'd experienced, and to listen to others.

The club was supposed to be over at four o'clock, but that night we stayed until almost seven, having freestyle battles and sharing poems. I remember being asked by one of the student leaders if he could get a ride home. Here I am in this car, at seven at night, talking about his poems and about what he wanted from his life. I think the joy he felt in receiving my advice was the same joy I felt in just being there to listen.

I dropped him off at his apartment. As he got out of the car, he gave me a look that I will never forget. He said, "Thank you, Mr. Howard. Nobody has really done this for me." I knew at that moment what my purpose was.

I'm a poet myself, and at the time, poetry was my focus. Just performing, being an artist, sharing my poetry. But I realized that day that my work with youth was my purpose. Even though I would get more fame or recognition as an artist, I had more fun teaching. My poems weren't here to just entertain; they were here to inspire, to challenge, even to agitate. To make people think.

After that day, I knew that Be the Voice was more than just a poetry club. Today, that student works as a program manager and instructor for my organization, Movement BE. Now he's realizing his purpose, inspiring other young people to find theirs.

You can do the same. You get what you think about most, and that means the only way to write the greatest version of yourself is to be able to hold that image of the real you in your mind and discard everything else. Your purpose will define that image and give you the shape of the story you're setting out to tell.

Let Purpose Be Your Guide

Most people never find their purposes. They go through life drifting, allowing other people to tell their stories, and they find themselves in careers and relationships that serve the purposes of others. They don't know who they really are because they've been conditioned or programmed to act a certain way. This leads to frustration, lack of drive, and depression.

This reality doesn't seem to depend on financial success. It's not uncommon to see an extremely successful millionaire who feels lost or frustrated because he or she never found a real purpose.

To find your purpose, think about what excites you. What are you passionate about? What's your talent? What skills do you have? What is unique about you, and how do you use that to serve others? That combination of skill and service is what purpose is.

Your purpose is the theme of your story. It's the reason your story exists. Without a purpose, your story has no flow, no direction. Your purpose is your guiding light. It's the reason you wake up every day. It's the reason you're compelled to achieve, or compelled to be compassionate, or compelled to live in this world when some days you want to give up. Only with purpose can you create that light to help others find their truth and their purpose.

Find Your Purpose

We're all connected, working to support each other, and each of us with our unique gifts can help those in need. Statistics have shown that serving others is what truly brings us happiness. Humans are genuinely selfless because we see ourselves in others. When we find the best way to give to the world, we find our purposes—and our happiness.

Purpose shows us that at the most challenging times, we can find the light through the darkness. School may teach us how to pass a test, but life teaches us our purposes. We all know that there will be ups and downs in life. What gets most of us through those challenging times is a purpose, a calling, a reason to do something. A feeling that we may not be able to fully explain because it's unique to us in our understanding of our life's mission.

When students ask me what their purpose is, I tell them to just pay attention. To be more observant of what's around them. Our purpose is there. It's been there since birth, since we were called here on this earth. We may have forgotten it because we were told to pursue things that were against our purpose, but we know when we find it.

So how do you do find your purpose?

You do it by finding what you love, what naturally allows you to be a gift to the world. Finding your purpose often comes at times of tragedy or times of surprise. You may find your purpose in a time of destruction or misery, after a horrible heartbreak, or the loss of a family member.

Your purpose is often something so much bigger than you that you have to grow into it. You have to become better to serve your purpose. That's why your story is always evolving—as are your opportunities for ways to serve and give to the world.

And when you live life on purpose, that's when you're living your best life.

The Dangers of Losing Purpose

When you lack a sense of purpose, on the other hand, it impacts every part of your life. It may be hard to get out of bed. It may be hard to eat the foods that nourish your body. It may be hard to do physical activity. When you feel like there's no meaning to life, or if you have nothing meaningful in your life, you feel nothing really matters.

Those who are not aligned with their purposes find themselves disconnected from who they are. They find love and gratitude only in the temporary things of life: possessions that will soon wither away or things that fulfill only for the short term. They have to be challenged to connect to something that is greater than them, and motivated to take on that you-versus-you battle.

Often other people try to give you meaning, try to tell you what your purpose should be, but that's impossible. This is something that only you can discover for yourself. Your purpose will become clearer to you the more you talk about it. It's not a word that most people use daily.

But it should be.

Gratitude Is the Way

Some people do things because they feel they have to. When you're living with purpose, on the other hand, you do things because you're called to do them. When you feel gratitude for the chance to do what you're doing, that's when you know that you're aligned with your purpose.

When you feel joy, when you feel blessed, notice what you're doing at that moment, at that time. What are the things that excite you, that make you feel good in the world? When you feel those feelings, be aware and see how it connects to your purpose.

Along the way, you'll connect with others who have also discovered their purposes, and that's where true alignment comes. Because we're only souls hoping to connect with each other, to help each other complete our life purposes, our life missions.

Purpose and Love

Most of us really don't understand love. We know conditional types of love. We know love at a surface level. But true love, unconditional love, love that we give even when we feel like we don't have it in us? That's our real purpose.

I remember when I went through my first heartbreak. It hit me like a big surprise. I had this person who was the love of my life, and suddenly everything fell apart. No matter how hard I tried to make it work to put the pieces together, I couldn't. I had lost the love of my life.

I had seen heartache in movies, but I had never felt that loneliness, that disconnect. It's a heavy place to be. Picking up the phone, knowing you can't call them, turning to tell them something and realizing they aren't there . . . During my breakup, I blamed myself for everything. If only I had done this differently, if only I hadn't made that mistake . . . I was beating myself up and not giving myself the love I truly deserved.

And then, this magical thing happened. All that love I wanted to give to her, I realized I had to give to myself.

That experience, which in that moment was so awful, showed me how important self-love really is. When you're reaching out across your bed, trying to find love and joy, you may only find a pillow. But you hold on to that pillow and you hug it tight, and when you want to cry and break down, it's okay to let it out to fill that pain.

And once you do, be mindful to quiet your mind. Quiet all the chaos and all the static and all the drama that's living up there, and find ways to just be. Your story is evolving, and in those big challenges, you may feel defeated. But it's about how you turn a negative situation into something positive. You find what it is that you can be thankful for, and you learn from the situation.

The best thing to propel you forward is helping others who've experienced what you've experienced. When you begin to tell other people about how to get out of challenging situations, you're living your purpose. The more you practice that, the more you give other people purpose, the more you constantly remind yourself of your own purpose, your own success. If you do that on a daily basis, you can heal and transform yourself while transforming others.

My first heartbreak wasn't easy, but it was the best thing that could ever have happened to me. I learned at that moment that our purposes are always changing and evolving as our stories continue.

On the road to your purpose, you'll find many challenges, but the only thing that will get you through it, the biggest thing that will get you through it, is love.

Loving yourself fully is what ignites your purpose. That self-love is a mirror to the world. When you can love yourself unconditionally, forgive yourself for past mistakes, and realize that the path you charted was the wrong direction.

Then you find yourself back on the road, full of love for who you are.

Your Purpose Belongs to No One Else

Understand that purpose is writing your story. Nobody has a story as you do, and nobody can ever have the same exact purpose as you do. The greatest experience in life is realizing how you uniquely can serve the world.

Your purpose is what gives you that momentum to get out of bed. It's what lights you up, what makes you feel or come alive in the world. Like all of us, you may get drained of energy day in and day out, but a purpose can recharge you so much that sometimes you even lose track of time. Your purpose becomes your fuel.

Some of us will realize on the journey of our purpose that ours is no longer society's perception of success. When we're dealing with envy and greed and all of these emotions that are connected to ego, when we're dealing with the need to be validated by society, we're not living our purposes. We forget who we are, and we find ourselves in a place of sadness, anger, and frustration. When we remove our egos or the need to be validated for society's definition of desire and success, we really get connected to who we are.

The reason many people feel unloved or like they're struggling in life is because they haven't found its meaning. Anytime I see people feeling lost, sad, or disconnected, I wonder how we can get them to connect to their love, their peace, and their gratitude so they can align with their purposes.

Because my purpose is to inspire generations to tell their stories before someone else does, I'm fueled every day to help young people find their voices. If I didn't have such a strong purpose, I would be drifting, not knowing who I am or what I'm called to do. I would be allowing other people to write their stories for me, allowing other people to give me a temporary purpose. And that temporary purpose only lasts as long as I can sustain a character that's not truly me.

Your purpose is the theme of your story. It's the reason you've even decided to write it because you have something in you that nobody else can give a voice to. Don't let that story die within you.

Chapter 4

Intuition

"Grass doesn't try to grow, it grows. Birds don't try to fly, they fly."—Deepak Chopra

Questions You Don't Know to Ask

To tell your story, you need to trust your intuition.

In 2014, I worked at the Monarch School in San Diego. It's a school designed for students impacted by homelessness. I was asked to give an eight-week program helping youth tell their stories through poetry. My goal wasn't to remind them of their situation but to get them to be open, to share the stories they wanted to tell.

After that eight-week program saw great success, the school decided to hire me part-time for the full year. By the time the year was almost over, I was ready to leave and try something new. But literally the morning I planned to tell my boss that I was thankful but moving on, he called and asked me if I wanted to introduce Deepak Chopra to the students. Chopra would speak, and then I would lead the kids in a poetic meditation.

Here I was, prepared to leave the job, but something told me to hold on. So I made a decision to trust my intuition. Through that experience with Chopra, I connected with an organization called Sonima. They were so impressed with my poetic meditation that they asked me to do a series of poetic meditation sessions for their website.

At that time, I had no idea what poetic meditation even was. It was just something that came to me. It was intuition. Today, when you google poetic meditation, my videos are the first to come up. It's as if something guided me and told me that this was my purpose, and that I was meant to learn more about this work.

I often say that you get what you believe in, but how do you know what to believe in? How do you know what's true and what's just your ego fighting for space? You have to use your intuition to know which parts of yourself you should embrace and which parts you should fight.

The Essence of Your Being

When you connect with your true self and understand the spirit and essence of your being, you're tapping into your intuition. There's no need to force anything. When you get in tune with your soul, you realize that all you have to do is just be.

Much of the information out there is intended to program us for someone else's agenda. Many of us have been conditioned, from a very young age, with information that doesn't serve us. The goal isn't to try to unlearn everything that was taught to you. Instead—focus on what lights you up. Focus on what brings out your greatest joy.

You do that by connecting to your intuition. That's another way of describing your connection with your source, whether that's your God or a feeling that's within you, however you identify it.

It may be hard to explain, but each and every one of us has a gut feeling, a knowledge of something that nobody can understand but us. When you practice connecting with your soul, be it through meditation or jogging or anything else that gets you connected in your solitude, you become more aware of life around you and better able to judge the decisions in your life.

Just be.

This is the you-versus-you battle. This is where you begin to teach yourself how to trust yourself more. You already know who you're becoming. Just be.

Your Intuition Is within You

We have to learn to trust our first impulses. Many times, we're afraid of who we really are. That first thought, that first excitement, that intuition, it comes to us. But we don't trust it. Instead, we say, "No, I can't do that." "No, I can't accomplish that." "No, that's not possible." But that first thought was our intuition reminding us of how great we really are.

Close your eyes and imagine the greatest version of yourself. Picture your thoughts and actions. If you settle for the doubts and believe that your intuition was just a grand idea, you'll end up scaling that version of yourself down to something so much less than it could be—than *you* could be. But you have all the tools you need to achieve that grand vision. Once you start on the path, the path appears.

The only way to continue to discover it is to go within. You can connect with your intuition through the practice of being in the present moment. Be still and feel this moment, right now. Listen as the message comes to you. This is what finding your story is all about.

True communication with yourself is so ingrained that there's no word for it in the English dictionary. It's a vibration that's so high, that's so connected to your greatest joy, that it's unnecessary to take the time to label these feelings. Just be. Allow yourself to breathe. Practice taking deep breaths, practice focusing on all parts of your body, and listen to it. This is an experience only you can understand. You may talk to others about intuition, or how they may feel, but nobody understands yours as you do.

Learn to trust that feeling.

Intuition Is the Path Forward

Trusting your intuition is how you make decisions on a daily basis. That could be as simple as deciding what to eat, or as complex as deciding what job to take or whether or not to leave a job that's not good for you. Your body, and everything connected to you, will tell you the answer. You just have to learn how to trust it.

Trusting your intuition can tell you about the relationships in your life too. Some things seem great on the surface, but inside you know something doesn't feel right. When you think about your romantic partners, for example, you may have a strong physical attraction, but your intuition will tell you to not get distracted by just what's on the outside.

Intuition is about seeing things that are unseen.

It may not be clear to everyone else, and you can't point to it or explain your intuition to others, but it is all-knowing to you. Intuition is about trusting the timing of your life. You may have an idea or a spark of excitement, but when you practice trusting your intuition, you'll know exactly when to act on it.

Your intuition will give you all the resources and information that you need to fulfill your purpose. That's why you have to go on this self-discovery journey within yourself to connect to your intuition. There is nobody like you.

Ego versus Intuition

Sometimes we call our intuition our gut, a weird sign, or even a coincidence. When our ego gets involved, it wants to try to make sense out of everything, but those thoughts are based on the external world. They're based on what we've seen from the outside, what we've been taught.

When we don't follow our intuition, we're not following our purpose. We find ourselves caught up in temporary gains, whether that's wealth or other things that provide us with temporary joy. These things serve our ego, but have to constantly be refilled. Some of us find ourselves caught up in drugs and other bad habits, hoping to get that feeling of joy.

In February of 2016, I had the idea to create the Movement BE app. I had been doing a variety of successful workshops all throughout San Diego, and I wanted a way to connect my students. I decided I needed an app to let students write their poems digitally so they would be able to share them openly, in a creative space.

After giving a poetic meditation workshop one day, I met a woman who had a friend who developed apps. After I told her what I envisioned, she gave me some estimates. I found out that I needed at least $10,000 to begin. The next day, while I was in the shower—a great place to connect with your intuition, by the way—it came to me that I should start a GoFundMe. I had this ambitious idea, this huge goal: to raise $10,000 in ten days.

I knew that if I could connect with all of my Facebook friends and everyone I knew on Instagram and Twitter, even if every person gave just a little, I could easily get the amount I needed. The part of me that was scared, my ego, wanted more reassurance. It wanted a plan. What if it didn't work? What if I didn't hit my goal? My ego screamed that I would be so embarrassed, that I couldn't take the risk of failure. All these negative thoughts hit me.

But following my intuition, I got out of the shower that day, logged on to GoFundMe, created an account, and told my story. I explained that I needed to raise $10,000 to help youth tell their stories in a new digital area, and I launched it. We didn't raise it in ten days, but we raised it in fifteen. We got our $10,000, and the first version of the Movement BE app was born.

When I created Movement BE, I didn't realize I was creating a movement to just be. But following my intuition set the idea into motion.

So often, we ignore our intuition because we're afraid it's nothing but ego. Intuition has no fear, but the ego does. Our egos want to hold on to a perfect self-image, a need to be perceived in the world a certain way. Our intuition, on the other hand, is so big that it can't even connect with something so limiting.

Don't allow yourself to be clouded by your own noise. That's your ego trying to fulfill your need for validation. Intuition tells you how to listen more than you speak. It shows you that your next step is your best step. While ego tells you, "Get here and you will be happy," intuition tells you, "Just be, and you are happy."

It's a hard concept to grasp sometimes, but your intuition tells you that there's no need to stress or worry. Intuition is your guide. So when you get that gut feeling, when something is stirring within you, it's up to you to learn and understand clearly what it's telling you. Build something, and practice learning how to be in tune with yourself.

Everything else will reveal itself.

Practice Intuition

In my personal practice, I make sure to meditate daily so that I have a sense of who I am. I quiet my mind so I can allow my intuition to fill that space. Every day we're filled with so much information that it boggles our minds! And that's really what's blocking the roadway of our intuition.

How ironic it is that when you close your eyes, you're finally able to see! You're able to pause and stop repeating the same information that you already know. You're able to just listen so that the spirit that's guiding you gives you direction on the next step to make.

If connecting is a challenge, don't be hard on yourself. The beauty of this is that the more you practice, the more aware you become. Those who are guided by their intuition know that all is well. That all is love, even in the hardest times. Because their intuition is telling them that things get better, and that each day is just a new step in following their purpose.

Close your eyes, be still, and listen to your greatest teacher. Allow yourself to breathe, to be alive, to feel either as a human being, or as a spiritual being having a human experience.

In that space, you're never alone.

Chapter 5

Vision

"Make your vision so clear that your fears become irrelevant."—Anonymous

Destroy Stereotypes

When we're focused on a vision, we have to think big. But so many of us are limited by the perception of who we think we are.

This perception often comes from stereotypes that box us into categories, and these stereotypes allow somebody else to tell our stories. Often we have ideas about what we want, but discourage ourselves based on our races or ages or genders, or any other categories or labels that have created assumptions about what a person can or can't be or do.

I've personally dealt with stereotypes as a young African American man. My visions were based on what I saw: to be successful, I had to be a professional athlete or a hip-hop artist. It wasn't until I was in college, until I saw the first Black president of the United States, that I opened my eyes to see Black men with other occupations and careers, thriving beyond the stereotypes. But I still had to realize something important: that pushing my vision meant I didn't have to reinforce any stereotype based on the story that was written for me.

Those images of people who looked like me often gave me a limited view of who I could be. And often, I was inspired and excited by that limited view. I wanted to be Allen Iverson, the basketball player, because he was my hero growing up. But if all I knew was the NBA, how would I ever discover the rest of my story? When we don't know our vision and who we truly are, the stories and stereotypes created for us will often get used against us.

When I heard the statistic that one in three Black men would go to prison in their lifetime, some saw that as an opportunity to fix such horrific data, to change the system that made the statistic a reality. I saw it as psychological warfare. When I see another unarmed Black man killed by police and covered on news stations all around the world, some see it as a call to fight for justice. I see it as psychological warfare.

The media attacks our minds. It's one thing to understand the pain and struggle of a group, but it's another to constantly see that pain and struggle without any true justice being served. The Black man's story becomes a political agenda, and people don't even know what they're fighting for.

We don't realize that the images we see of ourselves, the way we're reflected in the media, becomes our reality if we don't know how to write a new story. It's up to us to have the confidence to write a story that hasn't been told.

That's not saying you should be oblivious to other stories that are happening in the world, but instead that you're focused on being the greatest PR person for your story. There's light in your story. There's healing in your story. You see that vision, even if nobody else can.

As a Black man, I was often taught, specifically in college, that I should be aware of White privilege. In my understanding of it, I was to acknowledge that White privilege exists and that there's inequity in the world. I was taught that it would be up to me to challenge and figure out how to change that for my own freedom.

But then I realized that if White privilege continues to be a disclaimer, the fear of being racist will soon have an inverse effect, creating more racism than it cures.

I realized I was trying to tell my story through the lens of acceptance—acceptance of my Blackness to White privilege, or acceptance of my Blackness to other societal labels of who I was supposed to be. I'm proud of my Blackness, but what's in me is deeper than any social construct.

We're all individuals trying to beat the stereotypes, to push against or fight against some invisible force when all we have to do is just be. That begins with a vision for you to believe in. It begins by seeing and acknowledging the very best version of yourself, and then using that vision to win the battle and project outward in everything you do.

Believe in Your Vision

The power of your vision comes from you, and only you. If you try to prove or get validation from some external source, it's only giving them your story and asking them to edit and revise it to their liking.

When you have the confidence to fully tell your story, you're unapologetic. Benjamin Disraeli said, "Never apologize for showing feeling. When you do so, you apologize for the truth." To be your greatest self, your goal is just to feel.

Be kind to yourself. Telling your story is about spreading light and positivity into the world.

We all have a unique vision, and it's connected to the chapters that we write in our life. But when we get caught up in all the conversations that have been created by propaganda, that have been created to condition and program the minds of people who cannot think for themselves, then we do become victims.

Failure happens if you continue to see tragedy and feel no possible solution. You start to tell yourself that's just the way it is. You enter a reality where people can control your mind. Think about a fast-food commercial. When you constantly see the advertisement of what you should be eating to feel cool, you consume more of that food, even if it's not healthy for you.

It's important to understand that even though they seem innocent, many of the things we watch and read often have an intent to challenge our minds. Sometimes that challenge becomes so forceful and so addicting that it consumes our minds and orders it to live in a vision and story that isn't ours.

Even my writing of this book has a goal: to encourage you to write your own story. It's up to you to question everything. My vision is not your vision. This is me, writing my story. Writing this book is healing for me, and I only hope that in the same way, it can be healing for you too. But you should only use this as inspiration, not as law.

When we understand that the stories around us only serve as ways to question our own, we begin to have a deeper awareness of what our vision is. The more we question, the more we discover. The more we discover, the more our stories expand, and our vision gets larger.

Psychological warfare is the you-versus-you battle. Everything that you see is a reflection of how you feel. So don't let people distract you from your vision.

Be a Founder

When your vision becomes strong, it can help other people. Being a true founder isn't about ego. It's not a drive to say you own or operate a business. It's about realizing that your vision, connected to your purpose, is to help and serve others. And your vision is so large that other people can fit their vision within yours. When your vision becomes clear, and you know what you have to do, becoming a founder is inevitable.

What that means looks different for each and every one of us. We all live in a society where we need resources, and whether we're able to turn our narrative into business for an actual company, founders of our stories.

Make sure you're always in line with your vision, always being truthful with your story. Hold the vision and trust the process. It may often seem like nobody hears your story and that nobody else can really see your vision.

But soon, that tipping point will happen, and all of the people you shared your story with will be inspired to share their stories too. And they'll tell other people that you inspired them, and in that way, your vision becomes part of theirs. No matter how long that story becomes, it's not about the number of chapters or pages. Every day, there's something new to write. So be happy wherever you are in your story.

When people don't hold on to their vision, they're not only hurting themselves. The world also misses out on a story that could help the sick, uplift the poor, end racism, support teachers, create harmony, raise kids, innovate technology, or any of the other things that create a better future for us all.

Being a founder is simply finding your story. Once you find it, tell it to as many people as you can, however you can. Remember that your purpose is found in your skills. It's how you use those skills to serve others that helps you create your grand vision.

Chapter 6

Resilience

"If your heart is broken, make art with the pieces."—
Shane Koyczan

Know Your Truth—and Speak It

In May 2014, I was asked to give the commencement speech at the Black graduation for San Jose State. This was my first big speech, and I was going to tell the Black graduates about Black excellence and that, despite the stereotypes, they made it. They were graduating, maybe as first-generation college students.

Speaking with passion, I talked about the power of the next generation—how these young people of color would be our new leaders and that they were changing the narrative. As I finished, the crowd stood up, giving me a standing ovation. I was pumped, and I knew that this was the beginning of a great speaking career.

Soon after the graduation, I was invited to a friend's graduation party. At the end of the night, my friend had to use the bathroom, but the club was already closed. He went around the building, and I waited for him out front. Three police officers noticed him peeing behind the building, and one of them grabbed him by the arm while the other two officers walked him to a police car.

The way they were handling him alarmed me. "Why are you treating him this way?" I asked the officers. They told me to back up, and I did, still questioning why all of this was needed. "Just give him a citation or a ticket." One officer felt I was interfering with his process. He grabbed me and threw me to the ground. Suddenly everything was happening so fast. He pulled out a baton and gave me three strikes to my arm and my leg. In a flash, he had handcuffs on me.

I remember lying there on the pavement, thinking, "Just hours earlier, I was on the greatest stage of my life, giving my first commencement speech." But there I was, on the ground, in handcuffs. My body was bruised all over.

I was released that next morning. When I finally got back to San Diego, I got a lawyer so I could charge the officers for how they treated me. But as soon as I did, the police sent a warrant for my arrest. I had to go to court in San Jose for my own beating, not as the plaintiff, but as the suspect.

I was on trial for a week. The officers said they were scared of me, even though I'm not the biggest person. I remember sitting there, trying to convince a jury of who I was. Seeing these officers twist my story into something untrue.

When I was on the stand, I looked the prosecutor in the eye as she questioned my character. She said that maybe I just wanted to cause trouble. I told her how police treat people of color and how the system has incarcerated young Black men like me at disproportionate rates. I talked about the many issues of injustice that people of color have to face.

In that moment, I was proud of my crime.

Toward the end of the week, the judgment came back: guilty. I remember one lady juror who said that while she felt I had resisted arrest, the excessive force wasn't necessary. She didn't think it was fair that, because I was charged with resisting arrest, the police's behavior wasn't questioned. If I had been found innocent, I could have turned around and charged them for excessive force. But since the jury found me guilty, I couldn't pursue any legal action.

It was through resilience that I walked through that court case. Even after being found guilty, I knew that I wasn't a guilty person. Because of those events, I started a program called *Know Your Rights*, where I brought on an attorney to work with students to teach them how to interact with law enforcement.

As a protagonist in my story, my goal is to live the truth. I knew on that court stand that I was telling my truth. It was at that moment I realized that the world may find you guilty, but as long as you have your truth within, you can't have any enemies. That's the power of resilience.

Telling your story isn't always easy, and believing in the best version of yourself can be a struggle when everyone around you is trying to force their narrative to overwrite yours. But when you have resilience, you can keep writing.

You can keep fighting your own indecision or fear. You can keep speaking the truth without being silenced.

Importance of Resilience

When you get knocked down, how quickly you're able to get back up shows how connected you are to your source, to your true powers. The resilient person can't stay down for long. They know that nobody outside can save them.

A resilient person holds on to their story. Despite their story's bad grammar and syntax, a resilient person can edit and revise the story themselves, no matter how long it takes. They hold on to their character, to their integrity as a protagonist. With resilience, your whole purpose is to show the imperfect human who can face adversity and continue to grow and become a better version of themselves.

If you don't have resilience, you let other people tell your story. You let other people knock you down, keep you down, and make you feel inferior. You allow them to control your narrative.

The challenge for you is to understand that whatever the adversity may be, no matter how big, you are the only person who can decide the magnitude of your difficulties. Once you realize that you're bigger than any obstacle, you don't need to make any problem or challenge bigger than you are. Only then can you begin to redefine the obstacles in your life.

Turn Negative into Positive

Life is like a crazy roller coaster. There will be ups and downs and all kinds of crazy turns, but you can't say to life, "Let me just get off this ride."

When you're resilient, you know that life will continue to hit you in the face, but like when you're on the roller coaster ride, you just put your hands in the air and enjoy the journey. It's all about perspective.

You know that you can't skip the struggle, but you don't have to identify it as a struggle. Instead, see it as part of your story. As a protagonist, the antagonist will always try to defeat you. The antagonist doesn't want you to reach your personal treasure, your greatest self. But being the main character of your story, you understand it's your resilience that gets you through every chapter.

When the plot thickens, your greatest enemy is yourself. When you see adversity, you look it in the eye. And as you continue to stare, you'll see your reflection and know the acronym FEAR—false evidence acting real. Use that knowledge to make yourself strong, to push through.

You have more power than you know. When you quiet your mind and connect with your soul, you'll be reminded of that. When challenges seem overwhelming, it's because you just put a microscope on them, making them bigger than they actually are. You're magnifying things until they seem like your greatest defeat, but in truth, they're simply roadblocks that you can push out of your way.

Now, some roadblocks may be harder to push. It may take more time to get through them. That's okay. They are all part of the journey. Enjoy the journey.

It's the greatest feeling when you are getting through those roadblocks, defeating the odds, overcoming all of the obstacles, and proving everybody wrong who said you couldn't make it. That resilience is those blood, sweat, and tears. It's working as hard as you can to have the greatest story ever written, because it's yours. It always has been.

Perseverance versus Resilience

We've talked a lot about resilience, but how does that compare to perseverance? Perseverance is about pushing through obstacles and continuing to fight through each battle. Resiliency, although connected to perseverance, is more about knowing. Everybody can have either perseverance or resilience or both, but it takes the person who is in full control and the author of their story to understand what resiliency is trying to tell them.

The resilient person knows that their story came from tragedy. They've had their back against the wall. Everybody believed that they would fail—because of where they came from, the neighborhood they grew up in, the color of their skin, or whatever other stereotype was placed on them. But despite every obstacle, they know they won't be defeated. That's resiliency.

The resilient person understands their emotions. They know that tears aren't a weakness, and they're able to cry through the frustration. They understand the power to just be.

The resilient person knows that their story is fuel for someone else's, and that's what keeps their power alive: realizing that this story needs to be told. Even through the dark times, they know that the next chapter in their life will make all the rest worth it.

It may sound simple, but it's important to understand that having resilience through great tragedy takes a lot of courage. What do we tell a person who's been in prison for thirty years for a crime that he didn't commit? What do we tell the person whose family has been killed by genocide? What do we tell the people who, no matter what they do, are denied an opportunity because of systematic racism?

I say that despite how big the adversity or difficult it may be, you're the only one who can define what that difficulty means to you. Resiliency isn't about measuring how great a wound is or how difficult it is compared to something else. The goal is about having peace within.

I know it may seem easier said than done, but that's why the challenge and the reminder is to just be. Nobody can give you the answer to your difficulties. I can't tell you whether your challenges are simple or extremely difficult to handle. Instead, it's up to you to allow whatever is coming up in your life to connect to how you feel about finding your way through your story.

When you do that, you realize that it was always about you. It was never about them anyway.

Don't Take the Easy Road

Resilience is also about staying true to your vision, even when another path seems easier. In the fall of 2017, I was selected as Entrepreneur of the Year by the San Diego Central Chamber of Commerce.

During the event, I shared my short speech, which was a poem about identity. I walked off the stage to take pictures with my award. A few members of the board, who were friends of mine, told me they planned to use my picture to create a proposal for how they could better raise money for people who look like me using a new online platform.

Suddenly I was in a terrible situation. While I knew I deserved the award, I questioned the intention behind it. My acknowledgment suddenly seemed like nothing but an opportunity for them to use me for a platform they created to give donations to minorities. I turned down the award and the money that came with it.

My girlfriend at the time was furious. We barely had enough to eat, and we were continuing to max out our credit cards. I ate cereal for dinner, night after night, just to save money. And here was this great opportunity, money dangled in front of my face, and I turned it down.

Taking that money didn't feel right in my soul. I didn't want to be part of a gimmick. I didn't feel it was true to what I believed in. I felt betrayed by these individuals because they hadn't been transparent with me.

I rejected the only opportunity for money that I had. But I knew I would still be running my organization with integrity. And because of that resiliency, our organization now has fee-for-service contracts with school districts. We also get donations, but through a platform that we find to be reliable and consistent with our mission.

It's in those tough times when you're struggling and you need any opportunity just to survive that a resilient person knows how to say no. In the long run, I was thankful I made that decision.

With resilience, you don't sell yourself short. You know that everything that glitters isn't gold, and that difficulty will be inevitable when you do take the road less traveled. But it'll be worth it in the end.

Chapter 7

Digital Innovation

"If not me, then who? If not now, then when?"—Hillel

Tell Your Story to the World

It's often true that adversity drives innovation. In March of 2016, Movement BE started giving workshops in Southwestern College "learning communities," giving extra support to students of color. Our program was a success that first month, and many students were excited.

Over the next four years, the movement grew rapidly. But in March 2020, the pandemic hit, and schools across the country shut down. All of our workshops were canceled.

We convinced the schools to move our workshops online. Using Zoom calls, students could come online, and we connected with them virtually, sharing our screens with the Movement BE platform on it, and taking students through the activities in a virtual space.

Typically, students would write their poems on paper and turn them in at the end of the workshop. After the pandemic hit, students were able to go online, create profiles, and participate in what was suddenly an interactive activity. As soon as students posted their own poems, they were given access to see the poems of their classmates. They could comment, like, and talk about the poetry.

Movement BE launched our first virtual open-mic showcase on Zoom. We gathered all of the poems that the students wanted to present, put them in a slideshow, and ran the open mic virtually. The online platform gave students the opportunity to leave comments and support directly after a student finished reciting their poem. It provided a space to hear responses in a way that had never been done before.

This success is a reminder that in today's age, with innovation, you can create something beautiful in difficult times, and that solution could be even better than your original plan.

We've entered the digital age, and that means finding new ways to tell our stories. Being able to tell our stories online opens us up to audiences from all over the world, and lets us tell our stories in ways that once would have been impossible.

So many stories are never told, or they have been told for us. But finally, we're living in a time when we can begin to shift the narrative. People finally have access to tell their own stories before others do, and thanks to new digital technology, they can spread those stories across the world. Technology helps us with the battle of you versus you by giving us new tools to connect with others and ourselves.

Technology Has Opened New Roads

When we look at the advent of social media in the last decade, it's obvious how important it's become to social movements around the globe. We've seen people mobilize to participate in elections and connect with presidential candidates. We've watched companies share information with their customers in new ways. We've even experienced firsthand the growth of movements and online petitions that raise awareness on a variety of issues.

The innovation that has come with digital technology allows us to move our stories faster than ever before. With just an idea, a laptop, and a Wi-Fi connection, any one person can share a story that can change the world.

When we as a society realized the power of digital technology, we realized all of the information that was hidden from us and the things that we weren't fully informed about. Just a simple Google search brings forward more information in the beat of a heart than an entire day at the local library.

We also identified the opportunities that weren't being given to certain groups of people. Now, those of us fighting for equality and equity are working to create digital technology that breaks down barriers. It's far more difficult to discriminate against those of us who are oppressed because we don't have to go through gatekeepers. We can do it ourselves.

Sharing Your Story Online

The future of technology is preparing young people to create the world that they want to live in, using innovation to begin to close the equity gap (the resources people need to be given in order to be equal) and amplify stories that are often unheard.

When I created the Movement BE app and platform, I knew that the youth we worked with were being introduced to technology at an early age. We wanted to use technology to get young people to write their poems and stories in an open space where they felt safe. Today, our students in Southern California can connect with students in Ghana or Japan, bringing them closer to being global students.

Stories that we would have never heard are now available at the tips of our fingers. Through the innovation of technology, we can much more easily find out more about who we are. We can then spread our stories across multiple platforms, inspiring people to understand the messages we want to share.

A Digital Voice for the Silenced

Never before have we lived in a time with access to so many stories all across the globe.

Digital technology and innovation are bringing the world together, and it's up to us to realize the power of this innovation. It's up to us to be a part of this grand, world-wide story. The internet has created a world that's moving in a direction that challenges the status quo. Suddenly, we have the power to shift the narrative, to be inclusive of all people regardless of race, religion, or socioeconomic background.

We see this with simple hashtags, whether it be for Black Lives Matter, women's rights, or other social causes that so many people care about. Hashtags give voice to mobilize and build a movement online. That awareness pushes into our major news media, pushes into classrooms, pushes into corporations, making people care about a story that may have been started by one single person.

And that person could be you.

Never underestimate the power of telling your story online. Never underestimate the opportunity to take something that exists in your mind and turn it into a tangible creation that can inspire millions of people around the world. Your voice matters, and with this new innovation of digital technology, you can effect real change.

Innovation allows us to tap into stories that have often been oppressed, voices that have often been silent. With it, we can open a stream of new creations that are good for all of humanity. When we look at today's innovators, we can see that instead of looking at problems and accepting them as is, these entrepreneurs used their minds to solve problems that nobody was able to solve before. They found new solutions through the right resources and networks of people.

They began to create.

Don't Be Afraid

Everything that we live by and do on a daily basis was created through innovation. From something as simple as the bed we sleep in, to the food we eat, to the traffic light we stop at on the way to work, our lives are defined and created by people who realized that these things were important.

Today, if you want to be innovative, all you have to do is question what's needed that doesn't yet exist. Then ask yourself, Could I be the person to create it?

We all have unique and creative abilities, and so many of us waste our talents because we feel like we're not good enough. But because we have unique stories, and nobody has a talent like ours, it is up to us to have the courage to innovate.

Innovation is extremely important, especially for the person who feels their story isn't being told. Is that person you? Instead of allowing others to create the world that you live in, you can create your own. You can be free from limitations set by people who tell you that this is the only way to do things. Remember, two plus three equals five, but so does one plus four. The more you begin to change how you look at things, the more the things you look at begin to change.

Innovation Is Everywhere

I've always believed if you can teach William Shakespeare in school, you can teach Tupac Shakur. They're both poets. The realization that students will relate to Tupac more than they do Shakespeare led us to the innovation of the hip-hop curriculum.

Many of the students we serve are big hip-hop fans, connected to the urban communities that they live in. So we decided to create hip-hop songs to teach students about social emotional learning (in other words, emotional maturity). We wanted to teach students how to deal with depression, understand what gratitude is, be aware of mental health, and all the other things that are often left out and replaced by the typical algebra or biology class.

When we first introduced Tupac's book of poetry, students didn't realize that one of their favorite hip-hop artists could be the source of inspiration to keep them in school. His most famous poem is about a rose that grew from a crack in the cement, showing the struggle of how something so beautiful can come from something so ugly. Tupac's poetry resonated universally with the students, regardless of their backgrounds or where they grew up. His poetry gave them courage in relation to who they were.

Understanding the power of the students' new courage, we created original songs that included former students of Movement BE. They gave voice to raps that spoke to the students directly and inspired them much more than the traditional poets taught in schools, giving students something modern they could relate to: poets and creatives who looked like them.

That innovation led us to understand narrative therapy and using poetry as an outlet for healing. Students saw that the artists they looked up to and admired often used music as their own personal therapy, and that the students could do the same. Today, our hip-hop curriculum brings in stories of the voices that are often unheard, which was the origin of hip-hop.

We found that opportunity because we continued to create, pushing and challenging each other to live in a world that we can all find support in.

When we are innovators, we understand that with repeated attempts to create something, the right way will eventually appear. Innovation will keep happening. As we continue to learn more about ourselves, we'll find resources we never knew we had, and we'll grow a network of connections to people who are there to help us.

Whatever is in your mind, whatever you can think to create, walk on the way, and the way will appear. All it takes is that one step.

Chapter 8

Leadership

"The first and best victory is to conquer self."—Plato

A Story Can Inspire Leaders

Our stories can be inspirational to others. In January of 2015, I started a group called Young Visionaries. My idea was to gather like-minded millennials and create a space where we could share and support each other. I started a private Facebook group and invited a number of friends and acquaintances. I began my first post, sharing with the group who I was and what my intention was for this community.

I challenged others to give intros, sharing their bios and what they hoped to get out of this group. Numbers began to grow as I invited different visionaries who I felt were leaders within their communities. Soon they began to invite others. Our Young Visionaries Facebook group was building a network of some of the most talented twentysomethings across the country.

Since we had already met online, the next step was to find out how we could meet in person. That spring, I hosted meetups in San Diego, Los Angeles, and the Bay Area. I partnered with a friend, and we booked venues in each of these cities and put out a call to the young visionaries within our network.

This was one of the first ways I realized that I could lead people by telling my story. In simply sharing who I was and my purpose, I inspired other people to share their stories as well. As we moved our gathering from online to our physical space, we saw the stories of people connecting in person, creating opportunities for collaboration, and finding out how our leadership could show up for the projects that we wanted to create.

When you tell your story authentically, you acknowledge your own greatness. You fight that battle against yourself and see the power inside. Doing that opens you automatically to be a leader because you acknowledge that you have something worth sharing with others.

Leadership Starts Within

We think of leadership as a quality of leading others, but the truth is that everyone has the opportunity to lead—starting with themselves. On a personal level, this is the you-versus-you battle.

Leadership on a personal level is asking yourself, Am I leading the story that I want to live, or am I allowing my ego the false perception of being liked so that I can please others and be a follower in my own life? Am I avoiding living up to my true purpose?

Leadership in your personal life is realizing that even within yourself, you have to take responsibility for your mistakes. When it's you versus you, there's no one around other than yourself to blame. In that space, you're allowed to just be. The leader within you already knows who they are.

When you're caught up in ego and a false perception of yourself, it's easy to be led by the media and all of the other stories that are trying to tell you who you are. When following your purpose and seeing your vision through, the first step is to be connected to the leader within yourself. That leader has always been there, crying out, asking you to accept who you are.

Get Started as a Leader

Leadership in its beginning stages can seem difficult because getting people to believe in your vision takes guts. You need the courage to believe in yourself. A leader can't build a team until they get that first follower, someone who sees their authenticity. That first follower sees the leader, with their crazy idea, their big dreams, and their goals to change the world, and the courage and vision of that leader speaks to something in the follower.

That first follower will give you the confidence to expand your leadership skills. It's amazing that somebody else believes in this crazy idea you have. As you continue to expand your vision, the more you invest and pour into the people who start to follow you, the more you realize that the movement you're building creates a ripple effect.

As you inspire one person to tell their story, their story inspires others to tell theirs, and it continues.

Leadership Allows You Ownership

When telling your story, you have to become the leader of it. This is extremely important: not only do people try to tell your story for you, but sometimes they allow you to tell your story—only to take it from you. Leadership is about holding on to your story even when the allure of money and fame pushes you toward selling it to another leader. You don't want to find yourself giving your story away to another leader and ending up following *them* to figure out what *your* next chapter is.

Remember, nobody can tell your story as well as you can. You are its author. You continue to write it, and you become the best leader for yourself.

Don't give people the opportunity to appropriate your story, turn your authenticity into a gimmick, or simplify your struggle for the sake of profit. We see this happen all the time, and people don't realize that leading their own stories is the only way they connect to their purposes and the sources of who they really are. There is no dollar amount, there is no opportunity, there is nothing externally in the materialistic world that is worth giving your story away for someone else to lead.

When you do, they revise it, make edits, and delete chapters of your story. They change it in order to appeal to how others want you to fit within *their* story. You are the main character, the protagonist, on a search for your personal treasure. When you give your story away, you give those people opportunities to, instead, make you the antagonist of your own story.

So many of us are following the wrong people, trying to get our stories from them, and hoping they will soon appreciate us for who we are. But that's never their intent. When you take back the power and become the leader of your story, you'll be reminded that nobody, even your closest family and friends, even with good intentions, can lead your life story like you can.

It may be hard, and there may be difficult times. You may wish that you could give your story away, hoping that somebody else can take away your sorrows and your pain. But it is your story. We talked about resilience: it is up to you to hold on, to continue to claim the pen that is yours. When other people try to tell your story as a leader, they don't do you justice. They can't embody the message in the tone that represents who you authentically are. They invalidate your experience and limit your imagination.

Don't let somebody make you the villain of your own story. The story that you lead will always be within you. It is always there and always will be.

Learn from Your Mistakes

Remember Young Visionaries, the successful Facebook group I started? Well, despite its early success, about a year later, Young Visionaries died out. Our online space changed from a private group into a public group, and so many people were invited in that our online network got filled with spam and posts not related to our original purpose.

It was one of my first big lessons as a leader. Because instead of taking responsibility and trying to figure out our next steps, I ran away.

That Young Visionaries group is still on Facebook. Some people still post things they want to sell, or information on related events, but there's no authentic leadership. The group isn't what I meant it to be. But I don't see Young Visionaries as a failure. I see it as a great learning opportunity for my next venture. Because of everything that I learned while I led Young Visionaries, I became the best leader I could be for my organization Movement BE. I took responsibility to lead my team. And now I help lead youth to become the best leaders they can be.

I ran away from Young Visionaries because I was embarrassed. I hadn't yet learned to take responsibility for my mistakes, to show my face, and apologize when I was wrong or needed help. So instead of going back and fixing things, I left a number of people clueless on what was next for Young Visionaries. It was really unfortunate. If I could only have let go of my ego, I would have seen that there were other great leaders in the group who could have helped to support the movement. I didn't have to do everything myself.

Authentic Leadership

Leadership is about being authentic. Today, with a better understanding of what went wrong, I'm inspired to become a better leader. I still push the idea behind Young Visionaries, but now it's to create networking events in different cities for emerging leaders. As I lead in this new chapter, I will take the new skills I've learned and create a system that's sustainable. We'll have a plan, we'll be organized, and more than anything, I'll be honest about what I'm capable of as a leader and where I need my team to support me.

You have to see failure as a learning lesson to become better. As you lose people on your team, you'll find others to join you. No leader is perfect, but people believe in authenticity. Though a leader may not have all the skills when they first start, people are willing to trust a leader who's transparent.

Along the journey, authentic leadership becomes about making the people around you feel good, despite all the difficulties that you might be facing. Great leaders give their team courage, which gives them strength. Great leaders speak to people about where they can be, not where they are. And especially not where they *think* they are.

Leadership isn't necessarily about reaching a certain destination or leading people to a certain point, where they'll suddenly be happier and thankful to you. Leadership is about understanding the essence to just be. It's about allowing people to see the leader within themselves and giving them the courage to smile through the toughest days, enjoy the journey, and stay excited.

With true leadership, we're reminded that the service of making people feel great about themselves is our purest joy.

Chapter 9

Sustainability

"Wealth consists not in having great possessions, but in having few wants."—Epictetus

Get Rid of Your Hamburger Budget

Growing up, I was always told, "You shouldn't eat steak on a hamburger budget." Instead, I questioned why I would have a hamburger budget if I wanted to eat steak. Shouldn't I be aiming for what I truly wanted instead of settling for what I had?

In February 2017, I had just left a job where I was making $4,000 a month. Because it was Black History Month, many organizations were interested in my story about what Black history meant to me. When they asked me how much I would charge for a one-hour speech, I blurted out $5,000 . . . and they accepted. How is it that at a job I didn't like, I earned $4,000 a month, but to tell my authentic story in forty-five minutes, I could make $5,000?

It was unreal. I remember telling my parents, and they said I ripped off the organization. But I saw the truth: that I was worth that money. It began to shift the way I saw money and made me realize I had to decide what my worth was. That first success gave me the confidence to set $5,000 as my speaking rate. I knew I would get more opportunities like that.

Some speakers charge as much as $20,000 for a twenty-minute speech, and I believe that's in my future. And because I believe this, and put it out into the world, I'm able to sustain the story that I want to tell. I feel the power in being able to challenge myself to receive money based on the service, the product, that I'm selling.

I know that at the end of the day, if I want to make more money, I can decide to serve more people and create a product that can be useful to a number of people. Then I can vibrate at the level that matches my true worth, continuing to be the owner of my story, writing and directing it the way that I see it going for my future.

Sustainability is all about having the resources you need to tell your story so no one else steals that opportunity and tells your story before you can. When you claim your greatness and believe you're worthy of it being supported, you'll be able to set out financial goals that provide you the sustainability you need.

Financial Freedom

No one is teaching financial literacy in our schools. Our relationship to money is often one of fear—fear of not having enough. That analogy to the hamburger budget speaks to how many people are raised. We're taught that we have to accept crumbs or things that are less than what we really want.

If we change our definition of money and begin to see it as something that's helpful—a resource that allows us to follow our purpose and vision—then we can change the narrative of how money impacts our lives. We're taught that it's the rich versus the poor, and although huge gaps do exist, money in your life is relative. The amount of resources and money somebody else has in their story shouldn't affect what you need to continue yours.

I used to think that money was the root of all evil. I saw how that could be true for other people: the destructive way they would use money or put profit over people could be alarming. But I learned that doesn't have to be how I treat money. When I realized that my goal was to have financial freedom, I realized I needed to redefine my relationship with money. I wanted to figure out how I can do everything my heart desired and fulfill my purpose without having to worry about how much it would cost.

To some, that may seem like a privilege. "Easy for you to say," you might think. But why can't that be your story? So often, we limit our potentials because it costs too much. Instead of saying "I can't afford this," why don't we ask, "How can I afford this?" Challenge yourself to realize that money is just numbers, and attached to those numbers is the energy that you put behind it. It's a practice of being comfortable with realizing the abundance that is meant to be in your life.

We just have to believe we're worth it.

What Is Sustainability to You?

This isn't about figuring out how to become the next millionaire or even billionaire. This is about asking yourself what financial resources you *actually need* relative to your story. Without any comparison to what others may make, what resources will make you the happiest? What do you need to sustain your story?

I used to think I needed to make a certain amount of money to make me happy. I realized that my goal was actually to have enough to fulfill my purpose and to support others in helping them with theirs. In the spring of 2019, Movement BE started our program with Primetime, an after-school program serving elementary and middle school students that worked in partnership with the San Diego Unified School District. When they asked me how much my program cost, I had no idea how much to charge.

This was my first time working with elementary and middle school students, and it was my first time charging for a ten-session after-school program. I was scared because I didn't want them to reject the program because the price was too high. For days, I battled with how much I should charge.

I decided to meditate on it, giving myself the time and space to feel what it would be like if I received this amount of money.

Coming out of that meditation, I felt great. I picked a number, acting like I had received the money already. When I told them the price of the program, they responded quickly, easily accepting my offer. I was surprised—no need for negotiation, just an automatic, "Yes, that amount works." I realized immediately that I had sold myself short. I wasn't charging what I was really worth because I lived in the fear that I had to accept crumbs or discount my prices so people would appreciate and respect my work.

A year later, they asked us to do the Primetime program again. They offered us the same price per school, but with an added component of giving assemblies at an extra nine schools. But now, I better understood that what you seek is seeking you. I was no longer scared of my prices. I knew I was worth it. I told them what the new services would cost—and they agreed.

Being able to ask for what I was worth, when the opportunity was given, allowed me to be sustainable in operating my organization. Sustainability is planning for the future, making sure that you have all the resources necessary to keep your operations moving.

Growing up, I was taught to find a good job, buy a house, get married, and save for retirement. But the more I realized my own personal story, the more I understood that my whole goal wasn't to be a slave to a job, or to be dependent on certain ways of how to make money. For me, it was never about the money. It was always about my freedom—freedom to travel, freedom to write, freedom to just be. Being able to tell my story unapologetically and having the resources to support that. To live my truth and not to have to give away my story for a paycheck.

Financial Literacy Is a Skill

Challenge yourself to get educated about financial literacy. In school, you may have learned algebra, geometry, and even statistics, but it's doubtful you were educated about money. Most people haven't been. They don't know how money actually works, and that's why they continue to work for money instead of letting money work for them.

The more you educate yourself, the more you gain confidence in your relationship with money, giving you the ability to see things from a different perspective. Financial education is a personal discovery. Whether you're reading a book or taking a class, your investment in your financial success is personal to you. You can't ask anybody else how much you need: only you know the answer to that. Overcoming your fears of finance is about understanding the energy you feel in connection to money.

Think about the things that you want to do without the price tag attached. Feel yourself doing those things, accomplishing the best parts of your story. See how you feel. Let yourself get excited about that vibration, and don't worry about the cost. What you imagine and feel on the inside can come to life in your reality the more you practice and believe.

If in your mind you're vibrating a certain feeling about money, and open to that without any limitations, your mind will show you other ways to connect to that vibration. Potentially, it will show you answers to how you can receive that money in your life.

Change Your Mindset

In order to receive the resources we need, we have to change our emotions around money. Some may say, "I can't make a certain amount of money because, for someone like me, that's not possible." And you're right. He who says he can, and he who says he can't, are usually both right.

This is a you-versus-you battle, and you can make every argument in the book against why you can't be financially successful. But at the end of the day, it's totally up to you.

I can spend all of my energy finding arguments about why I can't make a certain amount of money or why other people make a certain amount of money, or I can spend my energy on focusing on my financial success. I can direct my thoughts to how I can make the money that's relative to me.

Financial freedom, to me, is about writing my story with authenticity. When people change their stories for paychecks or bonuses or any type of gimmicks for extra dollars, they lose who they really are. We see it happen all the time. Thankfully, some people will realize no amount of money is worth their souls.

So be intentional about how much money you want to make and why, but don't limit yourself. This is about sustainability for your story, so you can pass it down through the generations. It's about creating generational wealth.

It's my hope that my grandkids and their grandkids will be able to tell their stories unapologetically. I want them to feel free to be themselves because I had the courage to confront my fear of money. Because of me, they won't be trapped in a job where they have to be a slave to someone else's story—all because I had the courage to teach my community about financial literacy.

Chapter 10

Wisdom

"We do not attract what we want, but what we are."—James Lane Allen

Education Is a Process

I recently stumbled on a book called *Frequency: The Power of Personal Vibration* by Penney Peirce. The book talks about our frequencies and how fear vibrates on one level and love vibrates on another. This was one of the first books that I finished in a single day. This concept of frequency spoke to me—how it's connected to energy, and how we all have a certain vibration around us and match with other people and things with the same frequency.

I discovered that I could raise my frequency, and I didn't need any external stimuli to do that. It could all be from within. And the best thing I could do in raising my frequency was to feel good in the moment. But how could I feel good now if I didn't have something on the outside telling me or showing me how to feel good? I highlighted multiple pages throughout the book, taking time to pause to understand concepts on a deeper level. Then I began to apply each chapter to my life.

They say one book can change your life, and this book definitely had a huge impact on mine. This book showed me that I was on the right path with a lot of things I was already thinking, and it elevated my thoughts to another level. Once your mind expands to a new dimension, it never goes back to its old ways.

This book has become my greatest teacher. It reminds me to just be. I used to think that I needed to know all of these facts or miscellaneous information to prove I'm smart, or to say that I'm an expert in some type of industry. Eventually, I realized the greatest opportunity to learn and gain wisdom has no report card or diploma. I often reread the highlights of the book, knowing that motivation for me is a daily reminder, and I become wiser each time. This is something that nobody can take away from me.

That book changed my life, and I'm hoping it will do the same for you, giving you the ability to imagine and to see the magnitude of your true story. Who you are is so big, but you limit yourself when you don't gain the wisdom to become the best person you can be. Education is, and always has been, the key to freedom. Don't underestimate it.

You Have the Answers

The best education is self-education, and each day you'll grow wiser about how to become a better version of yourself. Who can write your life story better than you can? Just be. Allow your story to flow naturally. When you have writer's block and are trying to figure out the next page, or how to end a chapter in your life, and you can't seem to find the words to get you through this obstacle, just be. Pause, be still, and take time to search within.

By finding time to meditate and be mindful, I realized what I already knew. I'm in love with nature. I love eating food that feels good for my body. I enjoy laughter, the innocence of children, traveling to new places. These are my learning experiences. Discovering all the possibilities of life within is so different than what we're taught in formal education. Formal education tells me that once I get this degree or earn this certificate, I will be fulfilled. But there's a difference between knowledge and wisdom.

Though I'm proud of my college degree and the formal education I've received, nothing can replace the education of self. In that authenticity, you become connected to the source, whether you call that God or whatever spiritual higher power you may believe in.

Wisdom is knowing and being able to feel and sense things around you. Once you do that, you can feel the energy in choosing the right friends, connecting to the right job opportunities, and understanding your health and your body. This is the wisdom of getting to know yourself and loving every part of yourself.

Wisdom Isn't Knowledge

Growing up, much of what I am was from somebody else's perspective. There were so many things I later had to unlearn or change the way I looked at. So many people don't educate themselves on how to become better writers of who they are and thus don't know how to write their stories. Instead, they accept the teachings of their hunters, of their oppressors. They give their stories away, allowing their histories to forever be told by their oppressors, rather than educating themselves to discover their true histories.

Growing up as a Black American in school, the first thing I learned about my history was slavery. I felt like I was in bondage, trying to escape. Although slavery in America ended in the mid-nineteenth century, I still suffered from the struggle of my ancestors. Rightfully so, because there's still a fight for equality. But in educating myself, I discovered that people of my skin complexion were kings and queens in ancient Egypt. I learned about Mansa Musa, a Black man just like me, who was the wealthiest man during the Middle Ages.

There's no wonder that I grew up wanting to be Martin Luther King, Jr. or Malcolm X. That's what I was taught about in school. But if I were just limited to their perspectives, I wouldn't have been able to embrace all of the potentials that I am. People try to erase history or cover it up by telling a different story. But when you connect to *your* truth, you will find *the* truth.

Look within Yourself

At one school, the Movement BE program worked with elementary-aged, at-risk youth. I was asked to teach the kindergarten and first-grade group. I spent most of my time with these young kids doing chants. I would say something out loud and ask them to repeat it, and then we would add dance and other movements to our chant. The goal was to inspire these young kids to feel good about who they are.

One day, for our first chant, I said, "I am the greatest," and the kids repeated, "I am the greatest."

"I can do anything," I said, and the kids repeated, "I can do anything."

I said, "As long as I'm living," and they said, "As long as I'm living."

"I can be anything!" I yelled, and they shouted, "I can be anything!"

"I can be anything!" I repeated and told them to yell it as loud as they could. Their shouts filled the whole room. "I can be anything!"

But then I moved to a different chant. "I love myself!" I shouted. And the kids shouted, "I love myself!"

All but one. He yelled, at the top of his lungs, "I hate myself!"

I tried again. "Repeat after me. I love myself!"

All the kids repeated, "I love myself!" But that one kid insisted, even louder, "I hate myself!"

The other kids heard him and giggled and tried to tell him that he said the wrong words. But he knew what he was saying.

After class, I talked to the boy one-on-one. I tried to lead this one five-year-old boy to love himself. I looked him in the eye and said, "Please repeat after me. I love myself." But he just said, "I hate myself." I said, "Please. I love myself." He repeated, "I hate myself."

This young boy was impacted by homelessness. He was the youngest of five kids. When he got picked up that afternoon, I saw how his older siblings picked on him. They pushed and shoved and punched him, and he acted like everything was just okay. No one had taught him to love himself. No one had taught him to look in the mirror and see someone who was worth something. That day, I learned that no school would be able to teach that boy to love himself.

True wisdom is a you-versus-you battle, and it's all about learning to have the courage to find love within yourself. Other people can show you the way, or try to save you, but it's up to you to accept the challenge of loving yourself unconditionally.

Like that child, we've been told lies that make us hate ourselves. We find comfort in those lies, and we end up looking for more lies so we can find temporary happiness in appreciating ourselves. Instead, we need to turn the channel and tune into what makes us feel like our greatest selves unapologetically. Nobody can teach us about that type of love. Like this child, screaming "I love myself!" has to be authentic.

There's a quote by the poet Rumi I've always found inspiring:

When I run after what I think I want, my days are a furnace of stress and anxiety; if I sit in my own place of patience, what I need flows to me, and without pain. From this I understand that what I want also wants me, is looking for me and attracting me. There is a great secret here for anyone who can grasp it.

In telling your story, the great secret is to just be. What you seek is seeking you. So many of us get stressed about how to write the next chapter in our lives, but those who've gained wisdom understand that it is written. Allow your story to unfold by trusting the flow of your life.

The information you seek is not only seeking you, it's begging for you, wanting you, challenging you, showing up for you in ways that you could never imagine. When you have that self-love magnetized to you, attracting you to all the things that you love, giving you endless opportunities for discovering how you can love yourself more, filling your cup so that you can spread love to others, creating a ripple effect to show people how they can fulfill themselves with love—then we spread love all around.

Understand that everything is energy. I've realized that the more I vibrate on my highest level, the better I match other people, other opportunities that are also vibrating on that level. As you own your discovery, as you own your journey to discover your energy, learn how to vibrate at the highest level and meet high-vibrating people who will support your purpose.

Wisdom in your story is making analogies about your life lessons. Nobody else's. We can all be wise, because we all have unique stories. In understanding the wisdom of the stories that we tell, we connect to the key lessons in each part of our lives. Through this understanding, we gain the foresight to keep pushing our narratives or make changes if need be. But whatever we do, we don't stop telling our stories and sharing our wisdom.

Chapter 11

Closing

The Greatest Version of Yourself

We've arrived at the end of this book, but hopefully, it's a new beginning for you.

From here on out, you will no longer let others write your story for you. When you're writing the greatest story that has ever been told, which is coming from your inner understanding of self, people will undoubtedly pick up your story and read it. They have to. Because it was your story that needed to be told, to change the injustice in the world, to change the insecurity of so many people, just like you, who were feeling less about themselves. Your story can create a ripple effect.

By having the courage to tell it, you'll inspire so many people to find the story within themselves. That's something to celebrate. Just think what one story can do. It can move people to mobilize a movement for change, to help speak up for those who are less fortunate, to help amplify voices that often go unheard. *You* can do that. Your story, your message, your belief within yourself.

It won't be easy, but it's through your resilience that you continue to be the leader of your own life. When you understand your identity, and when it's led by your purpose, you understand the power to just be. Your intuition will guide you. Trust it. It sees your vision and understands the challenges you'll face along your journey. But in that persistence, you'll continue to innovate, adapt, and learn how your story fits into different mediums. You'll channel this to get your message across to the many people who need to hear it.

In that realization, you'll see that the telling of your story is connected to your own sustainability. When you don't tell your story, you can't sustain your life. When you let other people tell the story for you, you become part of their agenda to keep you inferior, to make you feel powerless. But when you understand that knowledge is power, and knowledge of self is wisdom, you can free yourself from that trap. You get what you think about most, so educate yourself on who you were called to be, so you can capture it in your mind and bring it to the light.

Continue to believe in the greatest version of yourself. You've been conditioned for so long to think less of yourself, to accept the crumbs, always in need of appreciation of others. But you can find balance. In the digital world that we're moving in, use social media as an influence, but also know when to turn your phone off to just be. Tell your story before they do. That you-versus-you battle you're fighting is the enemy within, telling you that you're not worthy. After all, if you're the author of your story, are you not also your greatest enemy? When you tell your story, you can say, I am the greatest and I own that.

Just Be

Join my tribe and tell your story every day. We're inspiring millions of youth across the world to just be. At http://movementbe.org, you can sign up to tell your story and connect with other youth across the world who have the courage to tell their stories too. If you need help telling your story, we offer a number of activities to support you in digging deep, whether that's overcoming your stress and anxiety or just trying to understand what gratitude might mean in your life.

Who knows? As we grow together, maybe we can join forces, pushing our stories together to create a new narrative, really believing that together we can change the world. I'm excited to get to know you. I look forward to reading your story, and I thank you for your courage.

It's amazing how much of my story has changed since the day seventy-nine LAPD officers shut down my party. Seven years later, my nonprofit organization partners with over eighty different schools and youth organizations across the country to help young people tell their stories. I work with those same law enforcement officers in some of the juvenile halls, where I work to inspire young people not to be victims of the justice system.

My story is really no different than yours. I'm living proof that when you turn your pain into purpose, the world gives you unlimited opportunities. That's true freedom. The freedom that you've been looking for to be yourself in a world that continues to oppress you. Because regardless of the struggles I've encountered, my story is about possibility despite the challenges. My story is about celebration despite the pain. My story is about overcoming again and again, and seeing the good throughout all the negativity in the world.

I've talked about the fact that you become what you think about most. The more you focus your energy on what lights you up in the world, the more you attract that energy.

Tell your story before they do, and remember: as the author of your story, it should be the greatest story ever written. Why would you write anything less of yourself?

You are the greatest, and you know that you're the greatest. Own that, and you're already halfway there.

ABOUT THE AUTHOR

Nate Howard is a professional speaker, poet, educator, and social entrepreneur.

A natural storyteller, Howard has performed at over sixty events, including TEDxSDSU, the Michelle Obama College Signing Day at the University of California, Riverside, and the Katapult Future Fest in Oslo, Norway. He was selected for the inaugural NBCBLK28 list as one of the "top 28 Black leaders in the nation under 28 years old," featured on the Today Show as one of the "Best and Brightest: Game Changers Making History," and honored in his hometown of San Diego as "Young Entrepreneur of the Year."

Howard tells stories as a form of social justice. He was inspired to share his truth after seventy-nine Los Angeles Police Department officers shut down a house party he was hosting at the University of Southern California. Realizing someone was attempting to tell his story for him, Howard sparked a movement against racial profiling, making the front page of the *LA Times.*

Howard went on to found the nonprofit organization Movement BE, where he serves as Executive Director. With the motto of "tell your story before they do" and a focus on poetry and self-expression, Movement BE helps change the narrative of underserved communities by giving youth the confidence to determine their own destinies. The movement has directly impacted thousands of students around the world.

Recognizing poetry as a means of self-expression, Howard challenges school systems to see its use as vital for the development of youth, giving them the courage to find their stories to challenge the status quo. Through Movement BE, he has taught poetry seminars on self-empowerment in over a hundred schools.

Howard has recorded his poetry on songs with artists Ty Dolla Sign, Kendrick Lamar, and Dr. Cornel West. He is a graduate of the University of Southern California.

Made in the USA
Monee, IL
16 August 2021